S0-BXW-795

Praying the
Rosary
with
Pope
Francis

Libreria Editrice Vaticana
United States Conference of Catholic Bishops
Washington DC

CONTENTS

How to Pray
the Rosary
(with Pope Francis)

Make the Sign of the Cross: *In the name of the Father,
and of the Son, and of the Holy Spirit. Amen.*

Invocation Prayer:

> *God, come to my assistance.*
> *Lord, make haste to help me.*
>
> *Glory to the Father, and to the Son, and to the*
> *   Holy Spirit:*
> *as it was in the beginning, is now, and will*
> *   be forever.*
> *Amen.*

* Holding the crucifix, say the *Apostles' Creed*.

* On the first bead, say an *Our Father*.

* Say one *Hail Mary* on each of the next three beads,
one for Faith, one for Hope, and one for Charity. Say the
Glory Be.

† For each of the five decades, announce the Mystery, then

† Read the biblical passage and Pope Francis' reflection,

† Say the *Our Father*,

† Say 10 *Hail Marys* while meditating on the Mystery,

† Say the *Glory Be*.

(After finishing each decade, some say the following prayer requested by the Blessed Virgin Mary at Fatima: *O my Jesus, forgive us our sins, save us from the fires of hell, lead all souls to heaven, especially those who have most need of your mercy.*)

† Having contemplated the five mysteries of the Rosary, say the *Hail, Holy Queen*, followed by this dialogue and prayer:

> V. *Pray for us, O holy Mother of God.*
> R. *That we may be made worthy of the promises of Christ.*

> *Let us pray. O God, whose only-begotten Son, by his life, death, and Resurrection, has purchased for us the rewards of eternal life, grant, we beseech you, that meditating on these mysteries of the most holy rosary of the*

Blessed Virgin Mary, we may imitate what they contain and obtain what they promise, through the same Christ our Lord. Amen.

Say the *St. Michael Prayer* and the *Litany of the Blessed Virgin Mary* (see Litanies section).

The *Our Father* and *Hail Mary* are prayed for the Pope's intentions to gain a *plenary indulgence* (see Indulgence section).

MYSTERIES
OF THE ROSARY

JOYFUL MYSTERIES

1.   The Annunciation
2.   The Visitation
3.   The Nativity
4.   The Presentation in the Temple
5.   The Finding of the Child Jesus After Three Days in the Temple

LUMINOUS MYSTERIES

1.   The Baptism in the Jordan
2.   The Wedding Feast at Cana
3.   The Proclamation of the Kingdom of God
4.   The Transfiguration
5.   The Institution of the Eucharist

SORROWFUL MYSTERIES

1.   The Agony in the Garden
2.   The Scourging at the Pillar
3.   The Crowning with Thorns
4.   The Carrying of the Cross
5.   The Crucifixion and Death

GLORIOUS MYSTERIES

. The Resurrection
. The Ascension
. The Descent of the Holy Spirit at Pentecost
. The Assumption of Mary
. The Crowning of the Blessed Virgin as Queen of
  Heaven and Earth

The four sets of Mysteries of the Rosary are traditionally
prayed on the following days:

Joyful Mysteries:	Mondays and Saturdays; Sundays of the Christmas Season
Luminous Mysteries:	Thursdays
Sorrowful Mysteries:	Tuesdays and Fridays; Sundays of Lent
Glorious Mysteries:	Wednesdays and Sundays (except Sundays noted above)

Rosary Prayers

The Sign of the Cross

In the name of the Father,
and of the Son,
and of the Holy Spirit. Amen.

Apostle's Creed

I believe in God,
the Father almighty,
Creator of heaven and earth,
and in Jesus Christ, his only Son, our Lord,
> (*At the words that follow, up to and including "the Virgin
> Mary," all bow*)
who was conceived by the Holy Spirit,
born of the Virgin Mary,
suffered under Pontius Pilate,
was crucified, died and was buried;
he descended into hell;
on the third day he rose again from the dead;
he ascended into heaven,
and is seated at the right hand of God the
Father almighty;
from there he will come to judge the living and
the dead.

I believe in the Holy Spirit,
the holy catholic Church,

the communion of saints,
the forgiveness of sins,
the resurrection of the body,
and life everlasting. Amen.

Our Father

Our Father, who art in heaven,
hallowed be thy name;
thy kingdom come,
thy will be done
on earth as it is in heaven.
Give us this day our daily bread,
and forgive us our trespasses,
as we forgive those who trespass against us;
and lead us not into temptation,
but deliver us from evil.

Hail Mary

Hail, Mary, full of grace,
the Lord is with thee.
Blessed art thou among women
and blessed is the fruit of thy womb, Jesus.
Holy Mary, Mother of God,
pray for us sinners,
now and at the hour of our death.
Amen.

Glory Be

Glory be to the Father
and to the Son
and to the Holy Spirit,
as it was in the beginning
is now, and ever shall be
world without end. Amen.

Fatima Prayer

(popular prayer after the Glory Be)

O my Jesus, forgive us our sins, save us from the fires of
hell, lead all souls to heaven, especially those who have
most need of your mercy.

Hail, Holy Queen (*Salve Regina*)

Hail, Holy Queen, Mother of Mercy,
our life, our sweetness and our hope.
To thee do we cry,
poor banished children of Eve.
To thee do we send up our sighs,
mourning and weeping in this valley of tears.
Turn then, most gracious advocate,
thine eyes of mercy toward us,
and after this our exile
show unto us the blessed fruit of thy womb, Jesus.
O clement, O loving,
O sweet Virgin Mary.

Prayer after the *Hail, Holy Queen*

V. Pray for us, O holy Mother of God.
R. That we may be made worthy of the promises of Christ.

Let us pray. O God, whose only-begotten Son, by his life, death, and Resurrection, has purchased for us the rewards of eternal life, grant, we beseech you, that meditating on these mysteries of the most holy rosary of the Blessed Virgin Mary, we may imitate what they contain and obtain what they promise, through the same Christ our Lord. Amen.

St. Michael Prayer
(popular prayer after the Rosary)

St. Michael the Archangel,
defend us in battle.
Be our protection against
the wickedness and snares of the Devil.
May God rebuke him, we humbly pray,
and do thou,
O Prince of heavenly hosts,
by the power of God,
thrust into hell Satan,
and all evil spirits,
who prowl about the world
seeking the ruin of souls. Amen.

JOYFUL MYSTERIES
(Monday and Saturday)

1. The Annunciation

Then the angel said to her, "Do not be afraid, Mary, for you have found favor with God. Behold, you will conceive in your womb and bear a son, and you shall name him Jesus. He will be great and will be called Son of the Most High, and the Lord God will give him the throne of David his father, and he will rule over the house of Jacob forever, and of his kingdom there will be no end." . . . Mary said, "Behold, I am the handmaid of the Lord. May it be done to me according to your word." Then the angel departed from her.

(Luke 1:30-33, 38)

Let ourselves be surprised by God

At the message of the angel, she does not hide her surprise. It is the astonishment of realizing that God, to become man, had chosen her, a simple maid of Nazareth. Not someone who lived in a palace amid power and riches, or one who had done extraordinary things, but simply someone who was open to God and put her trust in him, even without understanding everything: "Here I am, the servant of the Lord; let it be with me according to your word" (Lk 1:38). And he tells us: Trust me, do not be afraid, let yourself be surprised, leave yourself behind and follow me!

(Pope Francis, Homily, October 13, 2013)

2. The Visitation

During those days Mary set out and traveled to the hill country in haste to a town of Judah, where she entered the house of Zechariah and greeted Elizabeth. When Elizabeth heard Mary's greeting, the infant leaped in her womb, and Elizabeth, filled with the holy Spirit, cried out in a loud voice and said, "Most blessed are you among women, and blessed is the fruit of your womb. And how does this happen to me, that the mother of my Lord should come to me? For at the moment the sound of your greeting reached my ears, the infant in my womb leaped for joy. Blessed are you who believed that what was spoken to you by the Lord would be fulfilled." And Mary said: "My soul proclaims the greatness of the Lord; my spirit rejoices in God my savior."

(Luke 1:39-47)

Everything is God's gift

Take Mary. After the Annunciation, her first act is one of charity towards her elderly kinswoman Elizabeth. Her first words are: "My soul magnifies the Lord," in other words, a song of praise and thanksgiving to God not only for what he did for her, but for what he had done throughout the history of salvation. Everything is his gift. If we can realize that everything is God's gift, how happy will our hearts be! Everything is his gift. He is our strength!

(*Pope Francis, Homily, October 13, 2013*)

3. The Nativity

The time came for her to have her child, and she gave
birth to her firstborn son. She wrapped him in swaddling
clothes and laid him in a manger . . . Now there were
shepherds in that region living in the fields and keeping
the night watch over their flock. The angel of the Lord
appeared to them and the glory of the Lord shone around
them, and they were struck with great fear. The angel said
to them, "Do not be afraid; for behold, I proclaim to you
good news of great joy that will be for all the people. For
today in the city of David a savior has been born for you
who is Messiah and Lord. And this will be a sign for you:
you will find an infant wrapped in swaddling clothes and
lying in a manger."

(Luke 2:6-12)

Love made flesh

[Jesus] has entered our history. . . . He came to free us
from darkness and to grant us light. In him was revealed
the grace, the mercy, and the tender love of the Father:
Jesus is Love incarnate. . . . He is the meaning of life
and history, who has pitched his tent in our midst. The
shepherds were the first to see this "tent," to receive the
news of Jesus' birth. They were the first because they
were among the last, the outcast. And they were the first
because they were awake, keeping watch in the night,
guarding their flocks. . . . We bless you, Lord God most
high, who lowered yourself for our sake.

(*Pope Francis, Homily, December 24, 2013*)

4. The Presentation in the Temple

When the days were completed for their purification according to the law of Moses, they took him up to Jerusalem to present him to the Lord, just as it is written in the law of the Lord, "Every male that opens the womb shall be consecrated to the Lord" . . . Now there was a man in Jerusalem whose name was Simeon. This man was righteous and devout, awaiting the consolation of Israel, and the holy Spirit was upon him. . . . He came in the Spirit into the temple; and when the parents brought in the child Jesus to perform the custom of the law in regard to him, he took him into his arms and blessed God . . . Simeon blessed them and said to Mary his mother, "Behold, this child is destined for the fall and rise of many in Israel, and to be a sign that will be contradicted."

(Luke 2:22-23, 25, 27-28, 34)

Mary, hope of suffering peoples

[Mary] is the woman whose heart was pierced by a sword and who understands all our pain. As mother of all, she is a sign of hope for peoples suffering the birth pangs of justice. . . . As a true mother, she walks at our side, she shares our struggles and she constantly surrounds us with God's love. . . . As she did with Juan Diego, Mary offers [us] maternal comfort and love, and whispers in [our] ear: "Let your heart not be troubled . . . Am I not here, who am your Mother?"

(*Pope Francis*, Evangelii Gaudium, *no.* 286)

5. The Finding of the Child Jesus After Three Days in the Temple

Each year his parents went to Jerusalem for the Feast of the Passover . . . After they had completed its days, as they were returning, the boy Jesus remained behind in Jerusalem, but his parents did not know it. . . . After three days they found him in the temple, sitting in the midst of the teachers, listening to them and asking them questions . . . When his parents saw him, they were astonished, and his mother said to him, "Son, why have you done this to us? Your father and I have been looking for you with great anxiety."

(Luke 2:41, 43, 46, 48-50)

Mother of God

Our journey of faith is the same as that of Mary, and so we feel that she is particularly close to us. As far as faith, the hinge of the Christian life, is concerned, the Mother of God shared our condition. She had to take the same path as ourselves, a path which is sometimes difficult and obscure. She had to advance in the "pilgrimage of faith" (*Lumen Gentium*, no. 58). . . . To her let us entrust our journey of faith, the desires of our heart, our needs and the needs of the whole world, especially of those who hunger and thirst for justice and peace, and for God. Let us then together invoke her . . . "Mother of God! Amen."

(*Homily of Pope Francis, January 1, 2014*)

LUMINOUS MYSTERIES
(*Thursday*)

1. The Baptism in the Jordan

It happened in those days that Jesus came from Nazareth of Galilee and was baptized in the Jordan by John. On coming up out of the water he saw the heavens being torn open and the Spirit, like a dove, descending upon him. And a voice came from the heavens, "You are my beloved Son; with you I am well pleased."

(Mark 1:9-11)

Living a new life

We, by Baptism, are immersed in that inexhaustible source of life which is the death of Jesus, the greatest act of love in all of history; and thanks to this love we can live a new life, no longer at the mercy of evil, of sin and of death, but in communion with God and with our brothers and sisters. . . . It is precisely in the Sacrament whereby we have become new creatures and have been clothed in Christ. . . . Let us, then, ask the Lord from our hearts that we may be able to experience ever more, in everyday life, this grace that we have received at Baptism.

(*Pope Francis, General Audience, January 8, 2014*)

2. The Wedding Feast at Cana

On the third day there was a wedding in Cana in Galilee, and the mother of Jesus was there. Jesus and his disciples were also invited to the wedding. When the wine ran short, the mother of Jesus said to him, "They have no wine." . . . His mother said to the servers, "Do whatever he tells you."

(John 2:1-3, 5)

God's presence in the family

The true joy which we experience in the family is not superficial; it does not come from material objects, from the fact that everything seems to be going well . . . True joy comes from a profound harmony between persons, something which we all feel in our hearts and which makes us experience the beauty of togetherness, of mutual support along life's journey. But the basis of this feeling of deep joy is the presence of God, the presence of God in the family and his love, which is welcoming, merciful, and respectful toward all. And above all, a love which is patient: patience is a virtue of God and he teaches us how to cultivate it in family life, how to be patient, and lovingly so, with each other. To be patient among ourselves. A patient love. God alone knows how to create harmony from differences.

(*Pope Francis, Homily, October 27, 2013*)

3. The Proclamation of the Kingdom of God

After John had been arrested, Jesus came to Galilee proclaiming the gospel of God: "This is the time of fulfillment. The kingdom of God is at hand. Repent, and believe in the gospel."

(Mark 1:14-15)

No one is excluded from God's salvation

Jesus teaches us that the Good News, which he brings, is not reserved to one part of humanity, it is to be communicated to everyone. It is a proclamation of joy destined for those who are waiting for it, but also for all those who perhaps are no longer waiting for anything and haven't even the strength to seek and to ask. . . . Jesus teaches us that no one is excluded from the salvation of God, rather it is from the margins that God prefers to begin, from the least, so as to reach everyone. . . . He is calling us to go with him, to work with him for the Kingdom of God. . . . Let's let his gaze rest on us, hear his voice, and follow him! "That the joy of the Gospel may reach to the ends of the earth, illuminating even the fringes of our world" (*Evangelii Gaudium* no. 288).

(*Pope Francis, Angelus, January 26, 2014*)

4. The Transfiguration

[Jesus] took Peter, John, and James and went up the mountain to pray. While he was praying his face changed in appearance and his clothing became dazzling white. . . . While he was still speaking, a cloud came and cast a shadow over them, and they became frightened when they entered the cloud. Then from the cloud came a voice that said, "This is my chosen Son; listen to him."

(Luke 9:28-29, 34-35)

Jesus lives!

We have the hope of resurrection because he has opened to us the door of resurrection. And this transformation, this transfiguration of our bodies is prepared for in this life by our relationship with Jesus, in the Sacraments, especially in the Eucharist. We, who are nourished in this life by his Body and by his Blood shall rise again like him, with him and through him. As Jesus rose with his own body but did not return to this earthly life, so we will be raised again with our own bodies which will be transfigured into glorified bodies. . . . We believe that Jesus is Risen, that Jesus is living at this moment. . . . The power of his resurrection will raise us all.

(*Pope Francis, General Audience, December 4, 2013*)

5. The Institution of the Eucharist

Then he took the bread, said the blessing, broke it, and gave it to them, saying, "This is my body, which will be given for you; do this in memory of me." And likewise the cup after they had eaten, saying, "This cup is the new covenant in my blood, which will be shed for you."

(Luke 22:19-20)

The dinner table that is conformed to Christ

Jesus' gesture at the Last Supper is the ultimate thanksgiving to the Father for his love, for his mercy. . . . The Eucharist is the summit of God's saving action: the Lord Jesus, by becoming bread broken for us, pours upon us all of his mercy and his love, so as to renew our hearts, our lives and our way of relating with him and with the brethren. It is for this reason that commonly, when we approach this Sacrament, we speak of "receiving Communion," of "taking Communion": this means that by the power of the Holy Spirit, participation in Holy Communion conforms us in a singular and profound way to Christ, giving us a foretaste already now of the full communion with the Father that characterizes the heavenly banquet, where together with all the Saints we will have the joy of contemplating God face to face.

(Pope Francis, General Audience, February 5, 2014)

Sorrowful Mysteries

(*Tuesday and Friday*)

1. The Agony in the Garden

Then they came to a place named Gethsemane, and he said to his disciples, "Sit here while I pray." He took with him Peter, James, and John, and began to be troubled and distressed. Then he said to them, "My soul is sorrowful even to death. Remain here and keep watch." He advanced a little and fell to the ground and prayed that if it were possible the hour might pass by him; he said, "Abba, Father, all things are possible to you. Take this cup away from me, but not what I will but what you will."

(Mark 14:32-36)

A presence which accompanies

Christians know that suffering cannot be eliminated, yet it can have meaning and become an act of love and entrustment into the hands of God who does not abandon us; in this way it can serve as a moment of growth in faith and love. By contemplating Christ's union with the Father even at the height of his sufferings on the cross, Christians learn to share in the same gaze of Jesus. . . . To those who suffer, God does not provide arguments which explain everything; rather, his response is that of an accompanying presence, a history of goodness which touches every story of suffering and opens up a ray of light.

(*Pope Francis, Lumen Fidei, nos. 56-57*)

2. The Scourging at the Pillar

Pilate again said to them in reply, "Then what [do you want] me to do with [the man you call] the king of the Jews?" They shouted again, "Crucify him." Pilate said to them, "Why? What evil has he done?" They only shouted the louder, "Crucify him." So Pilate, wishing to satisfy the crowd, released Barabbas to them and, after he had Jesus scourged, handed him over to be crucified.

(Mark 15:12-15)

He gave himself for me

The Son of God offers himself to us, he puts his Body and his Blood into our hands, so as to be with us always, to dwell among us. And in the Garden of Olives, and likewise in the trial before Pilate, he puts up no resistance, he gives himself; he is the suffering Servant, foretold by Isaiah, who empties himself, even unto death. Jesus does not experience this love that leads to his sacrifice passively or as a fatal destiny. He does not of course conceal his deep human distress as he faces a violent death, but with absolute trust commends himself to the Father. Jesus gave himself up to death voluntarily in order to reciprocate the love of God the Father, in perfect union with his will, to demonstrate his love for us. On the Cross Jesus "loved me and gave himself for me" (Gal 2:20). Each one of us can say: "he loved me and gave himself for me." Each one can say this "for me."

(*Pope Francis, General Audience, March 27, 2013*)

3. The Crowning with Thorns

The soldiers led him away inside the palace, that is, the praetorium, and assembled the whole cohort. They clothed him in purple and, weaving a crown of thorns, placed it on him. They began to salute him with, "Hail, King of the Jews!" and kept striking his head with a reed and spitting upon him. They knelt before him in homage.

(Mark 15:16-19)

A King who loves

Jesus does not enter the Holy City to receive the honors reserved to earthly kings, to the powerful, to rulers; he enters to be scourged, insulted and abused . . . He enters to receive a crown of thorns, a staff, a purple robe: his kingship becomes an object of derision. He enters to climb Calvary, carrying his burden of wood. . . . Jesus enters Jerusalem in order to die on the Cross. And it is precisely here that his kingship shines forth in godly fashion: his royal throne is the wood of the Cross! . . . The King whom we follow and who accompanies us is very special: he is a King who loves even to the Cross and who teaches us to serve and to love.

(*Pope Francis, Homily, March 24, 2013*)

4. The Carrying of the Cross

And when they had mocked him, they stripped him of the cloak, dressed him in his own clothes, and led him off to crucify him. As they were going out, they met a Cyrenian named Simon; this man they pressed into service to carry his cross.

(Matthew 27:31-32)

Entering into the logic of the Cross

Following Jesus means learning to come out of ourselves . . . in order to go to meet others, to go toward the outskirts of existence, to be the first to take a step toward our brothers and our sisters, especially those who are the most distant, those who are forgotten, those who are most in need of understanding, comfort and help. . . . Living Holy Week means entering ever more deeply into the logic of God, into the logic of the Cross, which is not primarily that of suffering and death, but rather that of love and of the gift of self which brings life.

(*Pope Francis, General Audience, March 27, 2013*)

5. The Crucifixion and Death

It was now about noon and darkness came over the whole land until three in the afternoon because of an eclipse of the sun. Then the veil of the temple was torn down the middle. Jesus cried out in a loud voice, "Father, into your hands I commend my spirit"; and when he had said this he breathed his last.

(Luke 23:44-46)

The Cross of Christ, the Father's word of love

The Cross is the word through which God has responded to evil in the world. Sometimes it may seem as though God does not react to evil, as if he is silent. And yet, God has spoken, he has replied, and his answer is the Cross of Christ: a word which is love, mercy, forgiveness. It is also a judgment, namely that God, in judging us, loves us. Let us remember this: God judges us by loving us. If I embrace his love then I am saved, if I refuse it, then I am condemned, not by him, but my own self, because God never condemns, he only loves and saves. . . . Let us walk together along the Way of the Cross and let us do so carrying in our hearts this word of love and forgiveness. Let us go forward waiting for the Resurrection of Jesus, who loves us so much. He is all love!

(*Pope Francis, Way of the Cross at the Colosseum, March 29, 2013*)

GLORIOUS MYSTERIES
(Wednesday and Sunday)

1. The Resurrection

Mary Magdalene and the other Mary came to see the tomb.
And behold, there was a great earthquake; for an angel of
the Lord descended from heaven, approached, rolled back
the stone, and sat upon it. . . . Then the angel said to the
women in reply, "Do not be afraid! I know that you are
seeking Jesus the crucified. He is not here, for he has been
raised just as he said. Come and see the place where he lay.
Then go quickly and tell his disciples, 'He has been raised
from the dead, and he is going before you to Galilee; there
you will see him.' Behold, I have told you."

(Matthew 28:1-2, 5-7)

A really life-changing event

[The women] find the tomb empty, the body of Jesus is not
there, something new has happened. . . . Nothing remains
as it was before, not only in the lives of those women, but
also in our own lives and in the history of mankind. Jesus
is not dead, he has risen, he is *alive*! He does not simply
return to life; rather, he is life itself, because he is the Son
of God, the living God. . . . This is how the newness of
God appears to the women, the disciples and all of us:
as victory over sin, evil and death, over everything that
crushes life and makes it seem less human.

(Pope Francis, Homily Easter Vigil, March 30, 2013)

2. The Ascension

Then he led them [out] as far as Bethany, raised his hands, and blessed them. As he blessed them he parted from them and was taken up to heaven. They did him homage and then returned to Jerusalem with great joy.

(Luke 24:50-52)

Our humanity was taken to God

Jesus' earthly life culminated with the Ascension, when he passed from this world to the Father and was raised to sit on his right. . . . The Ascension of Jesus into heaven acquaints us with this deeply consoling reality on our journey: in Christ, true God and true man, our humanity was taken to God. Christ opened the path to us. He is like a roped guide climbing a mountain who, on reaching the summit, pulls us up to him and leads us to God. If we entrust our life to him, if we let ourselves be guided by him, we are certain to be in safe hands, in the hands of our Savior, of our Advocate. . . . The Ascension does not point to Jesus' absence, but tells us that he is alive in our midst in a new way. . . . In our life we are never alone: we have this Advocate who awaits us, who defends us. We are never alone: the Crucified and Risen Lord guides us.

(*Pope Francis, General Audience, April 17, 2013*)

3. The Descent of the Holy Spirit at Pentecost

When the time for Pentecost was fulfilled, they were all in one place together. And suddenly there came from the sky a noise like a strong driving wind, and it filled the entire house in which they were. Then there appeared to them tongues as of fire, which parted and came to rest on each one of them. And they were all filled with the holy Spirit and began to speak in different tongues, as the Spirit enabled them to proclaim.

(Acts 2:1-4)

The Holy Spirit, soul of mission

We contemplate . . . the outpouring of the Holy Spirit sent by the risen Christ upon his Church; an event of grace which filled the Upper Room in Jerusalem and then spread throughout the world. . . . The Holy Spirit draws us into the mystery of the living God . . . he impels us to open the doors and go forth to proclaim and bear witness to the good news of the Gospel, to communicate the joy of faith, the encounter with Christ. The Holy Spirit is the soul of *mission*. . . . It is the Paraclete Spirit, the "Comforter," who grants us the courage to take to the streets of the world, bringing the Gospel! The Holy Spirit makes us look to the horizon and drive us to the very outskirts of existence in order to proclaim life in Jesus Christ.

(*Pope Francis, Homily, Solemnity of Pentecost, May 19, 2013*)

4. The Assumption of Mary

A great sign appeared in the sky, a woman clothed with the sun, with the moon under her feet, and on her head a crown of twelve stars.

(Revelation 12:1)

Mary walks with us

The passage from Revelation presents the vision of the *struggle* between the woman and the dragon. The figure of the woman, representing the Church, is, on the one hand, glorious and triumphant and yet, on the other, still in travail. And the Church is like that: if in heaven she is already associated in some way with the glory of her Lord, in history she continually lives through the trials and challenges which the conflict between God and the evil one, the perennial enemy, brings. And in the struggle which the disciples of Jesus must confront . . . Mary does not leave them alone: the Mother of Christ and of the Church is always with us. She walks with us . . . Mary accompanies us, struggles with us, sustains Christians in their fight against the forces of evil.

(*Pope Francis, Homily, August 15, 2013*)

5. The Crowning of the Blessed Virgin as Queen of Heaven and Earth

Blessed be the God and Father of our Lord Jesus Christ, who has blessed us in Christ with every spiritual blessing in the heavens, as he chose us in him, before the foundation of the world, to be holy and without blemish before him. In love he destined us for adoption to himself through Jesus Christ, in accord with the favor of his will.

(Ephesians 1:3-4)

To be transformed by the beauty of God

The mystery of this girl from Nazareth, who is in the heart of God, is not estranged from us. She is not there and we over here. No, we are connected. Indeed, God rests his loving gaze on every man and every woman! . . . His gaze of love is on every one of us. The Apostle Paul states that God "chose us in him before the foundation of the world, that we should be holy and blameless before him" (Eph 1:4). We too, from all time, were chosen by God to live a holy life, free of sin. It is a plan of love that God renews every time we come to him, especially through the Sacraments. . . . By contemplating our beautiful Immaculate Mother, let us also recognize our truest destiny, our deepest vocation: to be loved, to be transformed by love, to be transformed by the beauty of God.

(*Pope Francis, Angelus, December 8, 2013*)

GRANT OF PLENARY INDULGENCE WITH DEVOUT RECITATION OF THE MARIAN ROSARY

What is an indulgence?

An indulgence is a remission before God of the temporal punishment for sins, whose guilt is forgiven, which a properly disposed member of the Christian faithful obtains under certain and clearly defined conditions through the intervention of the Church, which, as the minister of Redemption, dispenses and applies authoritatively the treasury of the expiatory works of Christ and the saints.

An indulgence is partial or plenary according to whether it removes either part or all of the temporal punishment due sin.

The faithful can obtain partial or plenary indulgences for themselves, or they can apply them to the dead by way of suffrage.

(*Manual of Indulgences*, *Norms* no. 1,
paraphrasing Paul VI's
Apostolic Constitution *Indulgentarium Doctrina*,
norm 1; and *Norms* no. 2-3)

Who can gain an indulgence?

In order to be capable of gaining indulgences one must be baptized, not excommunicated, and in the state of grace at least at the completion of the prescribed works.

To gain an indulgence, one must have at least the general intention of doing so and must carry out the enjoined works at the stated time and in due fashion, according to the sense of the grant.

A plenary indulgence can be acquired only once in the course of a day; a partial indulgence can be acquired multiple times.

(*Manual of Indulgences*, Norms no. 17, §1-2; no. 18, §1)

How to gain an indulgence?

To gain a plenary indulgence, in addition to excluding all attachment to sin, even venial sin, it is necessary to perform the indulgenced work and fulfill the following three conditions: *sacramental confession, Eucharistic Communion, and prayer for the intention of the Sovereign Pontiff.*

A single sacramental confession suffices for gaining several plenary indulgences; but Holy Communion must be received and prayer for the intention of the Holy Father must be recited for the gaining of each plenary indulgence.

The three conditions may be fulfilled several days before or after the performance of the prescribed work; it is, however, fitting that Communion be received and the prayer for the intention of the Holy Father be said on the same day the work is performed.

If the full disposition is lacking, or if the work and the three prescribed conditions are not fulfilled . . . the indulgence will only be partial.

The condition of praying for the intention of the Holy Father is fully satisfied by reciting one Our Father and one Hail Mary; nevertheless, one has the option of reciting any other prayer according to individual piety and devotion, if recited for this intention.

(*Manual of Indulgences, Norms* no. 20, §1-5, italics added)

Granting of a plenary indulgence to those of the faithful who recite the Marian Rosary

A *plenary indulgence* is granted to the faithful who

1° devoutly recite the Marian rosary in a church or oratory, or in a family, a religious community, or an association of the faithful, and in general when several of the faithful gather for some honest purpose;

2° devoutly join in the recitation of the rosary while it is being recited by the Supreme Pontiff and broadcast live by radio or television.

In other circumstances, the indulgence will be *partial*.

The rosary is a prayer formula consisting of fifteen decades of Hail Marys preceded by the Our Father, during the recitation of which we piously meditate on the corresponding mysteries of our redemption.[*]

Regarding the plenary indulgence for the recitation of the Marian rosary, the following is prescribed:

1. The recitation of a third part of the rosary is sufficient, but the five decades must be recited without interruption.
2. Devout meditation on the mysteries is to be added to the vocal prayer.
3. In its public recitation the mysteries must be announced in accord with approved local custom, but in its private recitation it is sufficient for the faithful simply to join meditation on the mysteries to the vocal prayer.

(*Manual of Indulgences*, *Grants* no. 17)

---

* In his 2002 Apostolic Letter *Rosarium Virginis Mariae*, St. John Paul II presented the five "mysteries of light," also called the Luminous Mysteries. They are generally included with the fifteen traditional decades of the Rosary, after the Joyful Mysteries and before the Sorrowful and Glorious Mysteries.

THE FIFTEEN PROMISES
GIVEN BY OUR LADY*

1) Whoever shall faithfully serve me by the recitation of the Rosary, shall receive powerful graces.

2) I promise my special protection and the greatest graces to all those who shall recite the Rosary.

3) The Rosary shall be a powerful armor against hell; it will destroy vice, decrease sin, and defeat heresies.

4) It will cause virtue and good works to flourish; it will obtain for souls the abundant mercy of God; it will withdraw the hearts of people from the love of the world and its vanities, and will lift them to the desire of eternal things. Oh, that souls would sanctify themselves by this means!

5) The soul which recommends itself to me by the recitation of the Rosary, shall not perish.

6) Whoever shall recite the Rosary devoutly, applying himself to the consideration of its sacred mysteries, shall never be conquered by misfortune. God will not chastise him in his justice. He shall not perish by an unprovided death, if he be just, he shall remain in the grace of God, and become worthy of eternal life.

7) Whoever shall have a true devotion for the Rosary shall not die without the sacraments of the Church.

) Those who are faithful to reciting the Rosary shall have during their life and at their death the light of God and the plentitude of his graces; at the moment of death they shall participate in the merits of the Saints in Paradise.

) I shall deliver from Purgatory those who have been devoted to the Rosary.

0) The faithful children of the Rosary shall merit a high degree of glory in heaven.

1) You shall obtain all you ask of me by the recitation of the Rosary.

2) All those who propagate the Holy Rosary shall be aided by me in their necessities.

3) I have obtained from my Divine Son that all the advocates of the Rosary shall have for intercessors the entire celestial court during their life and at the hour of death.

4) All who recite the Rosary are my children, and brothers and sisters of my only Son, Jesus Christ.

15) Devotion to my Rosary is a great sign of predestination.

---

* Promises given by Our Lady to Blessed Alan de la Roche, a Dominican father and promoter of the Rosary (1428-1475).

POPE FRANCIS'S PRAYERS TO OUR LADY

Prayer to Our Lady after the Profession of Faith

(May 23, 2013)

Mother of silence, who watches over the mystery of God,
Save us from the idolatry of the present time, to which
those who forget are condemned.
Purify the eyes of pastors with the eye-wash of memory:
Take us back to the freshness of the origins, for a prayer-
ful, penitent Church.

Mother of the beauty that blossoms from faithfulness to
daily work,
Lift us from the torpor of laziness, pettiness,
and defeatism.
Clothe pastors in the compassion that unifies, that makes
whole; let us discover the joy of a humble, brotherly,
serving Church.

Mother of tenderness who envelops us in patience
and mercy,
Help us burn away the sadness, impatience and rigidity of
those who do not know what it means to belong.
Intercede with your Son to obtain that our hands, our
feet, our hearts be agile: let us build the Church with
the Truth of love.
Mother, we shall be the People of God, pilgrims bound
for the Kingdom. Amen.

Prayer to Our Lady at Conclusion
of Recital of the Holy Rosary

(May 31, 2013)

Mary, woman of listening, open our ears; grant us to know how to listen to the word of your Son Jesus among the thousands of words of this world; grant that we may listen to the reality in which we live, to every person we encounter, especially those who are poor, in need, in hardship.

Mary, woman of decision, illuminate our mind and our heart, so that we may obey, unhesitating, the word of your Son Jesus; give us the courage to decide, not to let ourselves be dragged along, letting others direct our life.

Mary, woman of action, obtain that our hands and feet move "with haste" toward others, to bring them the charity and love of your Son Jesus, to bring the light of the Gospel to the world, as you did. Amen.

Prayer to Mary, Mother of the Church and Mother of our Faith

(Prayer to Our Lady at the Conclusion of the Encyclical Lumen Fidei, *June 29, 2013)*

Mother, help our faith!

Open our ears to hear God's word and to recognize his voice and call.

Awaken in us a desire to follow in his footsteps, to go forth from our own land and to receive his promise.

Help us to be touched by his love, that we may touch him in faith.

Help us to entrust ourselves fully to him and to believe in his love, especially at times of trial, beneath the shadow of the cross, when our faith is called to mature.

Sow in our faith the joy of the Risen One.

Remind us that those who believe are never alone.

Teach us to see all things with the eyes of Jesus, that he may be light for our path. And may this light of faith always increase in us, until the dawn of that undying day which is Christ himself, your Son, our Lord!

Act of Entrustment to Mary

(October 13, 2013)

Blessed Virgin Mary of Fatima,
with renewed gratitude for your motherly presence
we join in the voice of all generations that call you blessed.

We celebrate in you the great works of God,
who never tires of lowering himself in mercy over humanity,
afflicted by evil and wounded by sin,
to heal and to save it.

Accept with the benevolence of a Mother
this act of entrustment that we make in faith today,
before this your image, beloved to us.

We are certain that each one of us is precious in your eyes
and that nothing in our hearts has estranged you.
May that we allow your sweet gaze
to reach us and the perpetual warmth of your smile.

Guard our life with your embrace:
bless and strengthen every desire for good;
give new life and nourishment to faith;
sustain and enlighten hope;
awaken and animate charity;
guide us all on the path to holiness.

Teach us your own special love for the little and the poor,
for the excluded and the suffering,
for sinners and the wounded of heart:
gather all people under you protection
and give us all to your beloved Son, our Lord Jesus.

Amen.

Prayer to the Blessed Virgin Mary in Apostolic Exhortation *Evangelii Gaudium*

(November 24, 2013)

Mary, Virgin and Mother,
you who, moved by the Holy Spirit,
welcomed the word of life
in the depths of your humble faith:
as you gave yourself completely to the Eternal One,
help us to say our own "yes"
to the urgent call, as pressing as ever,
to proclaim the good news of Jesus.

Filled with Christ's presence,
you brought joy to John the Baptist,
making him exult in the womb of his mother.
Brimming over with joy,
you sang of the great things done by God.
Standing at the foot of the cross
with unyielding faith,
you received the joyful comfort of the resurrection,
and joined the disciples in awaiting the Spirit
so that the evangelizing Church might be born.

Obtain for us now a new ardour born of the resurrection,
that we may bring to all the Gospel of life
which triumphs over death.
Give us a holy courage to seek new paths,
that the gift of unfading beauty
may reach every man and woman.

Virgin of listening and contemplation,
Mother of love, Bride of the eternal wedding feast,
pray for the Church, whose pure icon you are,
that she may never be closed in on herself
or lose her passion for establishing God's kingdom.
Star of the new evangelization,
help us to bear radiant witness to communion,
service, ardent and generous faith,
justice and love of the poor,
that the joy of the Gospel
may reach to the ends of the earth,
illuminating even the fringes of our world.

Mother of the living Gospel,
wellspring of happiness for God's little ones,
pray for us.

Amen. Alleluia!

Prayer to Mary Immaculate

(December 8, 2013)

Virgin most holy and immaculate,
to you, the honor of our people,
and the loving protector of our city,
do we turn with loving trust.

You are all-beautiful, O Mary!
In you there is no sin.

Awaken in all of us a renewed desire for holiness:
May the splendor of truth shine forth in our words,
the song of charity resound in our works,
purity and chastity abide in our hearts and bodies,
and the full beauty of the Gospel be evident in our lives.

You are all-beautiful, O Mary!
In you the Word of God became flesh.

Help us always to heed the Lord's voice:
May we never be indifferent to the cry of the poor,
or untouched by the sufferings of the sick and those in need;
may we be sensitive to the loneliness of the elderly and
the vulnerability of children,
and always love and cherish the life of every human being.

You are all-beautiful, O Mary!
In you is the fullness of joy born of life with God.

Help us never to forget the meaning of our earthly journey:
May the kindly light of faith illumine our days,
the comforting power of hope direct our steps,
the contagious warmth of love stir our hearts;
and may our gaze be fixed on God, in whom true
    joy is found.

You are all-beautiful, O Mary!
Hear our prayer, graciously hear our plea:
May the beauty of God's merciful love in Jesus abide
    in our hearts,
and may this divine beauty save us, our city and the
    entire world.
Amen.

LITANIES IN HONOR OF MARY

Litany of the Blessed Virgin Mary
(Litany of Loreto)

Lord, have mercy	*Lord, have mercy*
Christ, have mercy	*Christ, have mercy*
Lord, have mercy	*Lord, have mercy*
God our Father in heaven	*have mercy on us*
God the Son, Redeemer of the world	*have mercy on us*
God the Holy Spirit	*have mercy on us*
Holy Trinity, one God	*have mercy on us*
Holy Mary	*pray for us*
Holy Mother of God	*pray for us*
Most honored of virgins	*pray for us*
Mother of Christ	*pray for us*
Mother of the Church	*pray for us*
Mother of divine grace	*pray for us*
Mother most pure	*pray for us*
Mother of chaste love	*pray for us*
Mother and Virgin	*pray for us*
Sinless Mother	*pray for us*
Dearest of mothers	*pray for us*
Model of motherhood	*pray for us*
Mother of Good Counsel	*pray for us*

Mother of our Creator	*pray for us*
Mother of our Savior	*pray for us*
Virgin most wise	*pray for us*
Virgin rightly praised	*pray for us*
Virgin rightly renowned	*pray for us*
Virgin most powerful	*pray for us*
Virgin gentle in mercy	*pray for us*
Faithful Virgin	*pray for us*
Mirror of justice	*pray for us*
Throne of Wisdom	*pray for us*
Cause of our joy	*pray for us*
Shrine of the Spirit	*pray for us*
Glory of Israel	*pray for us*
Vessel of selfless devotion	*pray for us*
Mystical Rose	*pray for us*
Tower of David	*pray for us*
Tower of ivory	*pray for us*
House of gold	*pray for us*
Ark of the Covenant	*pray for us*
Gate of heaven	*pray for us*
Morning Star	*pray for us*
Health of the sick	*pray for us*
Refuge of sinners	*pray for us*
Comfort of the troubled	*pray for us*
Help of Christians	*pray for us*
Queen of angels	*pray for us*
Queen of patriarchs and prophets	*pray for us*
Queen of apostles and martyrs	*pray for us*
Queen of confessors and virgins	*pray for us*
Queen of all saints	*pray for us*

Queen conceived without sin	*pray for us*
Queen assumed into heaven	*pray for us*
Queen of the Rosary	*pray for us*
Queen of families	*pray for us*
Queen of peace	*pray for us*

Lamb of God, you take away the sins of the world	*have mercy on us*
Lamb of God, you take away the sins of the world	*have mercy on us*
Lamb of God, you take away the sins of the world	*have mercy on us*

Pray for us, O holy Mother of God.
That we may become worthy of the promises of Christ.

Let us pray. Eternal God, let your people enjoy constant health in mind and body. Through the intercession of the Virgin Mary free us from the sorrows of this life and lead us to happiness in the life to come. Grant this through Christ our Lord. Amen.

Biblical Litany to Our Lady

Lord, have mercy	*Lord, have mercy*
Christ, have mercy	*Christ, have mercy*
Lord, have mercy	*Lord, have mercy*
Christ, hear us	*Christ, hear us*
Christ, graciously hear us	*Christ, graciously hear us*
God the Father in heaven	*have mercy on us*
God the Son, Redeemer of the world	*have mercy on us*
God the Holy Spirit, the Paraclete	*have mercy on us*
Holy Trinity, One God	*have mercy on us*
Holy Mary, Mother of God	*pray for us*
New Eve	*pray for us*
Mother of the living	*pray for us*
Descendant of Abraham	*pray for us*
Heiress of the promise	*pray for us*
Daughter of Zion	*pray for us*
Virgin soil	*pray for us*
Ladder of Jacob	*pray for us*
Burning bush	*pray for us*
Tabernacle of the Most High	*pray for us*
Ark of the Covenant	*pray for us*
Seat of Wisdom	*pray for us*
City of God	*pray for us*
Gate to the East	*pray for us*
Dawn of salvation	*pray for us*
Joy of Israel	*pray for us*
Glory of Jerusalem	*pray for us*
Honor of our people	*pray for us*
Virgin of Nazareth	*pray for us*

Virgin full of grace — *pray for us*
Virgin overshadowed by the Spirit — *pray for us*
Virgin giving birth — *pray for us*
Handmaid of the Lord — *pray for us*
Handmaid of the Word — *pray for us*
Humble and poor handmaid — *pray for us*
Wife of Joseph — *pray for us*
Blessed among women — *pray for us*
Mother of Jesus — *pray for us*
Mother of Emmanuel — *pray for us*
Mother of the Son of David — *pray for us*
Mother of the Lord — *pray for us*
Mother of the disciples — *pray for us*
Eager mother in the Visitation — *pray for us*
Joyful mother at Bethlehem — *pray for us*
Generous mother in the Temple — *pray for us*
Exiled mother in Egypt — *pray for us*
Anxious mother in Jerusalem — *pray for us*
Provident mother at Cana — *pray for us*
Resolute mother on Calvary — *pray for us*
Prayerful mother in the Cenacle — *pray for us*
Woman of the New Covenant — *pray for us*
Woman adorned with the sun — *pray for us*
Woman crowned with stars — *pray for us*
Queen at the right hand of the King — *pray for us*
Blessed are you who believed — *we love you*
Blessed are you who stored up the Word — *we thank you*
Blessed are you who did the
    will of the Father — *we honor you with grateful heart*

Lamb of God, you take away
    the sins of the world   *spare us, O Lord*
Lamb of God, you take away
    the sins of the world   *graciously spare us, O Lord*
Lamb of God, you take away
    the sins of the world   *have mercy on us*

Pray for us, O holy Mother of God.
    That we may be made worthy of the promises of Christ.

Let us pray. O God, Father of Christ our Savior, who
through the Blessed ever Virgin and tender Mother Mary
gave us the image of the Church, send us your Spirit to
help us in our weakness so that by preserving us in our
faith we may grow in love and walk together towards
eternal joy and salvation. Through Christ Our Lord. Amen.

ART CREDITS

Cover: Image of Pope Francis © Reuters/Tony Gentile; Image of Rosary, Shutterstock.

Inside:

p. 4   How to Pray the Rosary: photo © Kamira/Shutterstock.

p. 14   The Annunciation: by Masolino da Panicale, © Masolino da Panicale/National Gallery of Art.

p. 17   The Visitation: by Domenico Ghirlandaio, © The Gallery Collection/Corbis.

p. 18   The Nativity: by Fra Filippo Lippi, © Fra Filippo Lippi/National Gallery of Art.

p. 21   The Presentation in the Temple: *The Presentation of Jesus in the Temple* by James Tissot, © The Brooklyn Museum/Corbis.

p. 22   The Finding of the Child Jesus After Three Days in the Temple: by Ferdinand Prinoth/Shutterstock.

p. 25   The Baptism in the Jordan: *The Baptism of Christ* by Paris Bordone, © Widener Collection/National Gallery of Art.

p. 26   The Wedding Feast at Cana: *The Wedding at Cana* fresco by Giusto Menabuoi, © Gianni Dagli Orti/The Art Archive at Art Resource, NY.

p. 29   The Proclamation of the Kingdom of God: *The Lord's Prayer* by James Tissot, © The Brooklyn Museum/Corbis.

p. 30   The Transfiguration: by Giovanni Lanfranco, © Araldo de Luca/Corbis.